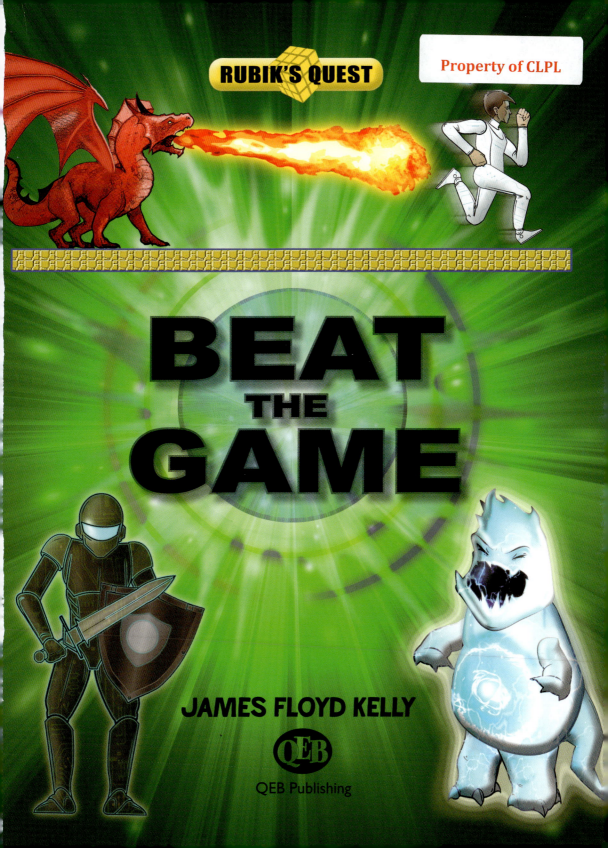

Cover Design: Rosie Levine
Illustrator: David Shephard
Editor: Amanda Askew
Designer: Punch Bowl Design
QEB Project Editor: Ruth Symons
Editorial Director: Victoria Garrard
Art Director: Laura Roberts-Jensen

Picture credits (t=top, b=bottom, l=left, r=right, c=center)

Science Photo Library 20br LAWRENCE LIVERMORE
NATIONAL LABORATORY/ SCIENCE PHOTO LIBRARY;
Shutterstock 46b 45tr Ruslan Semichev, 44c Mixov, 45tr
rvlsoft, 47tr Ingvar Bjork, 1 Veronica Lara; **Bigstock** 4 5 6 7
8t 12 17t 19b 20t 23t 27t 31t 33 35 37t 38 40 42t 43t
mr. Smith, 16t blackonix

First published in the US in 2014
by QEB Publishing, Inc.
3 Wrigley, Suite A, Irvine, CA 92618

www.qed-publishing.co.uk

A CIP record for this book is available from
the Library of Congress.

ISBN 978 1 60992 621 2

Printed in China

How to begin your adventure

Are you ready for an awesome adventure in which you must solve mind-bending puzzles? Then you've come to the right place!

Beat the Game isn't an ordinary book—you don't read the pages in order, 1, 2, 3 . . . Instead you jump forward and backward through the book as you face a series of challenges. Sometimes you may lose your way, but the story will always guide you back to where you need to be.

The story begins on page 4. Straight away, there are questions to answer and problems to overcome. The questions will look something like this:

IF YOU THINK THE CORRECT ANSWER IS A, GO TO PAGE 37

IF YOU THINK THE CORRECT ANSWER IS B, GO TO PAGE 11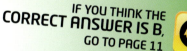

Your task is to solve each problem. If you think the correct answer is A, turn to page 37 and look for the same symbol in red. That's where you will find the next part of the story. If you make the wrong choice, the text will explain where you went wrong and let you have another chance.

The problems in this book are about programming and algorithms. To solve them, you must use your knowledge and common sense. Look out for the box above your head that shows you what level you're on and how many points you've collected. To help you, there's a glossary of useful words at the back of the book, starting on page 44.

ARE YOU READY?
Turn the page and let your adventure begin!

BEAT THE GAME

You're a computer game whiz and you've just received a strange email. It's inviting you to test your skills on a new computer game called Knight's Peril! You're about to start the game when a warning pops up.

Knight's Peril

COLLECT 26 CUBIES

BEWARE!

Once you start the game, you cannot leave until you complete it. Your mission is to collect 26 cubies throughout the game. The cubies will make a Rubik's Cube—your key to the exit, where you must defeat the Black Knight. Make your choice and press CONTINUE or CANCEL.

CONTINUE **CANCEL**

CLICK ON **CONTINUE** TO START YOUR **ADVENTURE** ON PAGE 16

Correct! A duplicate of you appears, before being taken to the RAM.

Back in the game, you find the doors are all locked. You look for a key and notice two chests labeled with letters. There's a plaque on the wall.

THE KEY IS INSIDE THE CHEST LABELED WITH THE NAME OF THE FASTEST AND MOST DURABLE DRIVE.

SSD   HDD

Which chest do you choose?

SSD
GO TO PAGE 33

HDD
FLIP TO PAGE 13

Wrong! You need to start the triangle by moving forward.

HAVE ANOTHER TRY
ON PAGE 18

Oh dear! A modulo doesn't collect viruses.

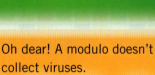

TURN BACK TO PAGE 40 AND TRY AGAIN

 Wise choice! ASCII, or the American Standard Code for Information Interchange, is one of the oldest codes used to represent characters on the screen.

You release the door and enter level one. The first cubie is above you. You touch it to collect it. How easy! There are lots of platforms above you, connected by ladders and ropes.

LEVEL 1

X 1

A smiley face pops up and speaks to you!

Reach the top to complete the level. Climb the ladders and ropes, but avoid the trapdoors. Beware—dragons will try to scorch you! Smiley faces like me will provide tips and hints.

You start to climb the first ladder, but the rungs suddenly disappear and you fall off. Rubbing your arm, you look up and words appear.

STEP ONTO THE RUNG MARKED BY THE NAME OF A PROGRAMMING LANGUAGE.

Which rung do you step on first?

BINARY

FORTRAN

X15

	101	HEAD TO PAGE 28
	⚛	FLIP TO PAGE 37
	🗡	GO TO PAGE 20

Correct! One terabyte equals 1,000 gigabytes (GB).

LEVEL 1 ×6

Very good.
Question two: What does USB stand for?

UNIVERSAL SERIAL BUS
GO TO PAGE 31

UNIVERSAL STORAGE BANK
FLIP TO PAGE 23

No! If you divide 8 by 2, there is no extra 1 left over.

TURN BACK TO PAGE 23 AND **TRY AGAIN**

Good! A loop repeats the instructions until the action is no longer required.

SPHERE tells you that the only way to stop the loop is to reprogram the code controlling the virus.

X = 1
WHILE X = 1 START LOOP
DESTROY ALL DATA 1s
DESTROY ALL DATA 0s
RETURN TO START LOOP
ATTACK NEXT RAM

You approach the monster and study the code.

Which part of the code do you reprogram?

CHANGE THE VARIABLE X TO 2
TURN TO PAGE 39

REMOVE "DESTROY ALL DATA 1s"
GO TO PAGE 23

Correct! Antivirus programs examine parts of a program or file for virus patterns. Once a virus has been found, it can be repaired or quarantined.

You open the file to activate it and a login window appears.

USERNAME: Administrator

PASSWORD: _ _ _ _ _ _ _ _

PASSWORD HINT:
WHO CO-FOUNDED MICROSOFT?

ANTIVIRUS

What do you enter?

BILL GATES
GO TO PAGE 43

STEVE JOBS
TURN TO PAGE 30

 No, an algorithm is far more important than a tune!

TRY AGAIN
ON PAGE 36

Wrong! A byte is made up of eight bits, so it isn't the smallest piece of data.

TURN TO PAGE 16 AND
RE-ENTER THE PASSWORD

 No, it's not called static current.

TRY AGAIN
ON PAGE 31

Great! SSL is a Secure Sockets Layer. It protects data over the Internet by encrypting it (putting it in a secret code) before it is sent.

Your sword double-strikes the Black Knight and he loses two lives! He's shocked—he didn't know about the programming you added to strengthen your sword and shield! He quickly answers his question correctly so you receive a strike—but your shield doubles in strength.

LIVES
5

LIVES
4

QUESTION 2:

WHICH NETWORK PROTOCOL IS USED TO SEND EMAIL?

FTP
GO TO PAGE 41

SMTP
HEAD TO PAGE 18

Bad idea! READ allows the corrupted data to communicate with you, but WRITE lets it make changes to your data.

TRY A **DIFFERENT SETTING**
ON PAGE 13

B Wrong! Loops, points, and slices have nothing to do with a disk drive's surface.

TURN BACK TO
PAGE 22 AND
TRY AGAIN

Correct! An algorithm is a set of instructions for performing an action. For example, an algorithm controls how an app works, telling it what to do next.

You pass through the portal into the CPU. An alarm is ringing loudly. A bright-red "1" character rushes over to you.

The CPU is overheating because the algorithm that runs it is wrong. If it gets too hot, the computer will crash and any unsaved data will be lost forever, including you!

Change the value of X so the CPU can cool down. Its temperature should never be above the value 100.

ALGORITHM TO SET CPU TEMPERATURE:

X = 2

IF X < 5 SET CPU_TEMP = 400

IF X > 5 SET CPU_TEMP = 100

You study the algorithm. What change do you make?

INCREASE THE **VALUE** OF X TO 6.
TURN TO PAGE 38

DECREASE THE **VALUE** OF X TO 1.
GO TO PAGE 16

Get real! HTML can only create items such as drop-down menus and text boxes.

BACK TO PAGE 28
TO TRY AGAIN

 Correct! EXECUTE and SAVE are both commands, but TIME = 9 is a variable. Variables can be identified by an equals sign.

You climb to the top platform, where 10 cubies are waiting for you! You can see a door saying EXIT. What an easy level! In your excitement, you step on a dragon's tail poking out of a trapdoor. The dragon roars and turns toward you with its nostrils smoking.

You jump up to hit a smiley face.

LEVEL 1

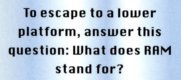 x 19

To escape to a lower platform, answer this question: What does RAM stand for?

 RANDOM-ACCESS MEMORY
GO TO PAGE 20

 **RAPID APPLIED MEMORY**
TURN TO PAGE 36

No, app isn't short for appliance.

TRY AGAIN ON PAGE 37

Incorrect! Hard disk drives (HDDs) contain moving parts that wear out over time.

TRY AGAIN ON PAGE 5

Correct! By following the instructions in the algorithm, you've landed on the correct final square. The force field disappears.

You carefully approach the disk in front of you, but SPHERE stops you.

Don't get too close or the disk's corruption might damage your data. Set your Data Permission to avoid data corruption.

RESET DATA PERMISSION

NO ACCESS

READ ONLY   READ/WRITE

What do you change your data permission to?

READ ONLY FLIP TO PAGE 30

READ/WRITE TURN TO PAGE 10

Well spotted! Brainiac is a made-up name for a computer.

You open the door to level three. Behind it is a bridge leading to another platform. You can see 5 cubies on the other side!

As you start walking across the bridge, a plank breaks— then another and another. You're stranded in the middle. The Master Programmer's voice fills the air.

The bridge represents the computer's power system. One false step and your computer will lose power —and it'll be game over for you!

The gameplay screen dims, showing the power levels have gone down. Oh dear! A screen drops down in front of you.

TO EARN NEW PLANKS AND BOOST THE COMPUTER'S POWER, ANSWER THE FOLLOWING QUESTIONS CORRECTLY. EACH INCORRECT ANSWER EQUALS A LOSS IN POWER.

WHAT IS THE UPS?

Think quickly. What do you say?

UNINTERRUPTIBLE POWER SUPPLY
TURN TO PAGE 31

UNIVERSAL POWER SYSTEM
GO TO PAGE 26

Colors flash before your eyes. You begin to shrink in size as you're pulled toward the swirling graphics . . . into the game!

As your vision returns to normal, you see a login screen before you.

LOG IN TO PLAY

USERNAME: *GAMER*
PASSWORD: . . . .

CLUE: SMALLEST PIECE OF INFORMATION THAT A COMPUTER USES

Which password do you enter?

BIT
HEAD OVER TO PAGE 26

BYTE
FLIP TO PAGE 9

No! To set the temperature to 100, you need to make X larger than 5, shown with X > 5. If you decrease the value of X to 1, the CPU will get even hotter. The CPU will stay at its current temperature if you do not make the right choice.

TRY AGAIN ON PAGE 11

Brilliant! Scratch uses drag-and-drop shapes that are placed in specific orders to create programs.

You reach the top platform again and head toward the exit. You try to walk through it, but an error pops up.

EXIT

LEVEL 1

x 19

Save and exit to next level

ERROR! RAM CANNOT SAVE LEVEL. CORRUPTION!

SPHERE appears to help you.

Time to go inside the computer again. A virus is attacking the RAM. Follow me along the Road to RAM.

SPHERE takes you along the road, but there's a roadblock in the way. A sign shows the detour routes.

TO FIND THE FASTEST DETOUR ROUTE, ANSWER THIS QUESTION:

Which command gives users choices that result in different actions?

✳ EXECUTE (TASK X)
TURN TO PAGE 42

? IF (SELECTION X) – THEN (TASK X)
GO TO PAGE 29

Good choice! The Input program means it's expecting to receive a 1 or a 0. The Output program will send out a 1 or 0.

The planks are repaired. You hurry to reach the other side, but stop quickly—the ropes are untying! The Master Programmer speaks again.

As if I'd make it that easy! Final power challenge. The following Python code is muddled up. Put it in the correct order to make the turtle robot draw an equilateral triangle.

A ROTATE RIGHT (60)
B MOVE FORWARD (100)
C ROTATE RIGHT (60)
D MOVE FORWARD (100)
E MOVE FORWARD (100)

Which order will draw a triangle?

ACBED
GO TO PAGE 31

BCDAE
HEAD TO PAGE 22

CAEDB
FLIP TO PAGE 5

No, memory chips don't have hooks!

TURN TO PAGE 29 AND TRY A **DIFFERENT OPTION** **?**

Yes! SMTP stands for Simple Mail Transfer Protocol and it's used to send email. POP is used to retrieve email.

You strike the Black Knight and he ends up with only 2 lives! One more double-strike and you win! The Black Knight answers his question correctly and strikes you a second time. Your shield doubles in value, but you lose a life.

QUESTION 3: WHAT IS A FIREWALL?

ANTIVIRUS PROGRAM
GO TO PAGE 39

INTERNET FILTER
FLIP TO PAGE 34

No, a virus is software that attempts to destroy data and copy itself to other computers.

TURN BACK TO PAGE 30 AND
MAKE ANOTHER SELECTION

Afraid not! Here's a clue: BASIC was created for beginner-level programmers.

TURN BACK TO PAGE 41
AND **TRY AGAIN**

You press the button X = 1, and the sword speeds toward the viruses, destroying them before they reach the RAM. The viruses are gone, and the RAM blocks appear to be functioning properly.

You return to the game, save the level, and enter level two. A message pops up.

LEVEL 2

x 19

MAKE A BACK-UP OF ALL CHARACTERS. CHOOSE THE CORRECT COMMAND.

It would be a good idea to make a back-up of yourself. That way you can't be accidentally deleted! Which command do you select?

MOVE
GO TO PAGE 38

COPY
TURN TO PAGE 5

Correct! RAM stands for random-access memory. It can store and retrieve a computer's data in any order.

You land on the platform below, just as dragon fire blasts the top platform. That was a close one!

You run to the closest ladder, but it keeps moving away from you.

 LEVEL 1 × 19

TO STOP THE LADDER, ANSWER THIS QUESTION:

WHICH PROGRAMMING TOOL USES COLORFUL BLOCKS THAT CAN BE DRAGGED AROUND ON SCREEN TO CREATE PROGRAMS?

SCRATCH
GO TO PAGE 17

PYTHON
HEAD TO PAGE 33

No, X15 is the name of a rocket-powered aircraft used by the U.S. Air Force.

TRY AGAIN ON PAGE 6

No! Univac was a mainframe computer first available in the early 1950s.

TRY AGAIN ON PAGE 33

Choose again! A DVD can usually hold 4.7 gigabytes (GB) of data, but another media type can hold more than five times that.

TRY AGAIN ON PAGE 31

Incorrect! EXECUTE is one of two commands in the list.

GO BACK TO PAGE 38 AND **TRY AGAIN**

LEVEL 3

x20

Yes, AC is converted to direct current, or DC. The electricity that travels along power lines into your home is AC. It is then converted to DC, which powers computers and other electrical devices.

Another plank appears and you step forward.

WHICH COMMAND INDICATES THAT A PROGRAM IS EXPECTING TO RECEIVE A 1 OR A 0?

OUTPUT
GO TO PAGE 36

INPUT
TURN TO PAGE 18

LEVEL 3 x20

Great job! You programmed the turtle to draw an equilateral triangle!

The ropes re-tie themselves. You reach the other side of the bridge and collect 5 cubies. Phew!

There's no door—only ropes that will take you down to a lower level. You start to slide down one, but it isn't secure so you fall with a thud.

SPHERE appears by your side.

> The ropes have become detached because there's a malfunction in the hard drive. You need to leave the game to fix it.

SPHERE takes you to the Hard drive Highway. A sign shows you which route to choose.

WHAT IS A DISK DRIVE'S SURFACE DIVIDED INTO?

A TRACKS, SECTORS, AND CLUSTERS.
TURN TO PAGE 32

B LOOPS, POINTS, AND SLICES.
GO TO PAGE 10

C QUARTERS, SEGMENTS, AND SLIVERS.
FLIP TO PAGE 28

Well done! Yes, the modulo command is used to calculate a remainder. For example, when 5 is divided by 3, the remainder is 2. 5modulo3 would return a value of 2.

The sword begins to glow. Another message appears on the blade.

To double the sword's power, reset the XtraBit variable. Give it a value that can be split into 2 equal numbers and leave a remainder of 1.

XTRABIT = ?

How do you complete the algorithm?

8

XTRABIT = 8
TURN TO PAGE 8

9

XTRABIT = 9
GO TO PAGE 38

Incorrect! You haven't followed the algorithm correctly.

GO BACK TO PAGE 32 AND **TRY AGAIN** **A**

Although that will stop the virus from destroying the 1s, it will continue to attack the 0s.

GO BACK TO PAGE 8 AND **TRY AGAIN**

Although USB drives are used for storing files, the letters USB stand for something else.

HAVE ANOTHER TRY ON PAGE 8

On the other side of the doorway is a spiral staircase. At the top, you meet a figure in black armor, holding a shield and sword.

Behind him is a glowing portal saying **EXIT THE GAME FOREVER.**

You have little time to think before he charges at you. You hold up your shield, ready to take the hit. But then you hear laughing.

Ha ha! Scared you! That's not how we duel. We may be dressed as knights, but we duel with brainpower. I challenge you to a Quick-fire Quiz Duel!

EXIT THE GAME FOREVER

He explains the rules. You take turns to answer quiz questions. For each correct answer, you strike your opponent. If you answer incorrectly, your opponent strikes you. For each strike, you lose a life. Six strikes and you lose!

A screen lowers. You will answer the first question.

QUESTION 1:
WHAT IS SSL SHORT FOR?

SECURE SOCKETS LAYER
GO TO PAGE 10

SECURE SOFTWARE LOOP
TURN TO PAGE 30

No, SAVE and another word are both commands. They tell the computer what to do next.

TURN BACK TO PAGE 38 AND **THINK AGAIN**

 No, the UPS acts like a large battery if the power goes out.

TURN BACK TO PAGE 14 AND **TRY AGAIN**

 Wrong! The () are used to put calculations in order. For example, in 2 x (5+3) the sum 5+3 is worked out first, then multiplied by 2.

$$2 \times (5 + 3) = 2 \times 8$$

TRY AGAIN ON PAGE 43

Login successful! The smallest piece of information a computer can use is a 0 or a 1. This is called a bit.

You find yourself standing on a drawbridge with two doors before you. You're in a castle computer game! An instruction flashes up.

OPEN THE DOOR MARKED BY ASCII CHARACTERS.

Which do you choose?

GO TO PAGE 6

TURN TO PAGE 42

Correct! App is short for application—a program that carries out a particular job. For example, a mobile phone app can show the local weather forecast.

LEVEL 1 x6

You jump over the dragon, grab three cubies and run to the end of the platform. A large ladder runs straight to the top of the level. You try to climb it, but some of the tiny dots in the image, called pixels, are corrupted so it disappears.

A voice booms out:

I am the Master Programmer. The game is corrupt because there are problems on your computer. Leave the game to fix them before the computer crashes and you are lost forever. SPHERE will guide you, if you can answer three questions. Question one: What is 1,000 gigabytes (GB) also called?

ONE PETABYTE
TURN TO PAGE 43

ONE TERABYTE
GO TO PAGE 8

 No! The antivirus will simply perform a scan, but it won't destroy future viruses.

GO BACK TO PAGE 43
AND **TRY AGAIN**

 The division symbol is not going to help! It will divide the shield's value in half every time it is struck.

TRY AGAIN
ON PAGE 38 9

Incorrect! Binary means made of two pieces. A binary digit, or bit, is a piece of information but not a type of programming language.

TURN BACK TO PAGE 6 AND TRY AGAIN

 Oh dear! Quarters, segments, and slivers are terms you'd use to divide a cake, not a disk drive.

TRY AGAIN ON PAGE 22

 Not that one! It will delete all data stored in memory, including you!

TURN TO PAGE 39 AND MAKE A DIFFERENT CHOICE

That's right! Malware tries to monitor your actions and send that information to the malware programmer. This slows everything down.

You'll need to repair the damage done by the malware by entering a code into the hard drive.

CODE CLUE: WHAT IS HTML USED TO CREATE?

INPUT ANSWER: _ _ _ _ _ _ _ _ _

 WEB PAGES
GO TO PAGE 42

 APPS
HEAD TO PAGE 12

Correct! IF–THEN gives users choices within a program. Each choice results in a different action.

You follow the diversion route. At the end of the road are four enormous RAM blocks, each one storing masses of Os and 1s. A monstrous creature is pulling parts of a RAM block away. It's the virus! The Os and 1s are all screaming for help.

RAM Block D

RAM Block C

RAM Block B

RAM Block A

Help us!
The virus is using a loop
to stay active.

But what is a loop?

IT IS USED TO **REPEAT** A BIT OF PROGRAMMING **CODE OVER AND OVER.** GO TO PAGE 8

IT IS USED TO **HANG** A PROGRAM ON A **MEMORY CHIP HOOK.** FLIP TO PAGE 18

Incorrect! Steve Jobs was an inventor who co-founded Apple Inc. in the 1970s.

TRY AGAIN
ON PAGE 9

 Incorrect! SSL does not stand for Secure Software Loop.

TRY AGAIN
ON PAGE 24

Good choice. The READ ONLY will allow the damaged data to communicate with you without making changes.

Now you're protected, you ask one of the unhealthy Os why it is sick.

We picked up software that works secretly within the hard drive. It has made us turn black and run slowly. Do you know what this software could be?

What do you say?

MALWARE
GO TO PAGE 28

VIRUS
TURN TO PAGE 19

Excellent! USB stands for universal serial bus. "Serial" means data is sent one bit at a time. "Bus" is an old computer term for the wires that data moves along.

BLU-RAY
GO TO PAGE 41

DVD
TURN TO PAGE 21

Lucky guess! Question three: Which media type can hold the most information?

LEVEL 1
x6

Incorrect! You can't start drawing the triangle by turning right 60 degrees.

TURN BACK TO PAGE 18 AND TRY AGAIN

That's right. The UPS can provide a computer with power for a few minutes should the main power source fail.

A plank appears on the bridge and you step forward. A second question appears.

THE POWER SUPPLY CONVERTS ELECTRICITY FROM AC, OR ALTERNATING CURRENT, TO WHAT?

What answer do you shout out?

DC, OR DIRECT CURRENT
TURN TO PAGE 21

SC, OR STATIC CURRENT
GO TO PAGE 9

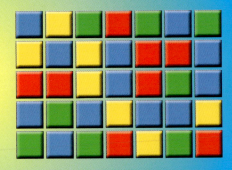

SECTOR

TRACK

CLUSTER

A Correct! A disk drive is made up of tracks (thin bands that run around the disk), sectors (chunks), and clusters (groups of individual sectors).

You follow the route and arrive at the hard drive—a silver disk. There is a cluster of black corrupted 0s.

You try to reach them, but you're blocked by an invisible force field. Suddenly the force field turns into a grid of colored squares.

TO DEACTIVATE THE FORCE FIELD, PRESS THE SQUARES IN THE RIGHT ORDER BY FOLLOWING THIS PROGRAMMING ALGORITHM.

1. START ON ANY GREEN SQUARE. IF YOU REACH A POINT WHERE YOU CAN NO LONGER FOLLOW THE ALGORITHM, START AGAIN ON ANOTHER GREEN SQUARE.

2. ALWAYS MOVE FORWARD ONTO A BLUE SQUARE IF THERE IS ONE IN FRONT OF YOU.

3. MOVE RIGHT ONTO A YELLOW SQUARE.

4. MOVE LEFT ONTO A RED SQUARE.

5. MOVE ONTO THE FINAL SQUARE IN THE ALGORITHM.

What color square do you end on?

ON A GREEN SQUARE
GO TO PAGE 23

ON A RED SQUARE
TURN TO PAGE 41

ON A BLUE SQUARE
HEAD TO PAGE 13

Well done! Solid state drives (SSDs) are fast, durable, and quiet because they have no moving parts that can become damaged.

You grab the key and a cubie from inside the chest. When you turn toward the doors, there's a message above them.

ONE DOOR WILL LEAD YOU TO THE NEXT LEVEL,
AND THE OTHER TO A DRAGON.

CHOOSE THE DOOR THAT IS NOT LABELED WITH THE NAME OF AN EARLY MAINFRAME COMPUTER.

Which door do you choose?

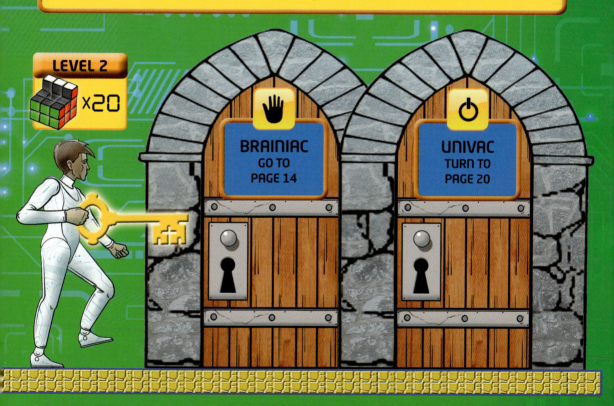

LEVEL 2
×20

BRAINIAC
GO TO
PAGE 14

UNIVAC
TURN TO
PAGE 20

Wrong! Python is a text-based programming tool, meaning you need a keyboard.

TRY AGAIN
ON PAGE 20

Correct! A firewall protects a computer by filtering Internet traffic. It blocks anything that is harmful to the computer.

You double-strike the Black Knight again. His life count turns to zero and his pixels disappear. You run toward the exit portal and the game swirls away from you.

Suddenly you find yourself sitting at your desk, staring at the computer screen. A message flashes across the screen.

WINNER!

YOU COLLECTED ALL 26 CUBIES AND DEFEATED THE BLACK KNIGHT.

YOU ARE THE BEST GAMER IN THE WORLD!

What a strange experience. But this confirms it—you really are the best gamer ever. You knew it!

No, RAM does not stand for rapid applied memory. It is a type of memory that can store data in any order.

GO BACK TO PAGE 12 AND **TRY AGAIN**

No, 1920 is far too early for video game inventions.

TURN BACK TO PAGE 42 AND **TRY AGAIN**

INPUT

OUTPUT

Wrong! Output means a 1 or a 0 will be going out of the program, not into it.

TURN BACK TO PAGE 21 AND **TRY AGAIN**

Correct! BASIC is one of the earliest, simplest programming languages.

The security cuboid lets you pass. You reach a glowing green portal.

TO ENTER THE CPU, PRESS THE CORRECT BUTTON.

WHAT IS A PROGRAMMING ALGORITHM?

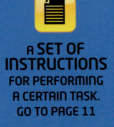

A **SET OF INSTRUCTIONS** FOR PERFORMING A CERTAIN TASK.
GO TO PAGE 11

A **TUNE THAT PLAYS** WHEN YOU START A PROGRAM.
TURN TO PAGE 9

Great choice! Fortran is a programming language, developed in the 1950s especially for scientific calculations.

You step on the correct rung and climb to the top, collecting two cubies on the way. Oh no! A dragon is walking toward you. You run toward a smiley face.

LEVEL 1

x3

To use a power-leap and jump over the dragon answer this question: What is the word "app" short for?

APPLICATION
GO TO PAGE 27

APPLIANCE
FLIP TO PAGE 13

Correct! OR operations use the II characters. For example "schools will be closed if there is rain OR snow" can be written "**R II S**." With OR operations, only one of the two conditions must be true (rain OR snow) for the effect (school closed) to take place.

The armor starts to glow and transfers to cover your body. It's time to face the Black Knight and win the game.

GO THROUGH THE DOORWAY
TO PAGE 24

Nice job! 9 can be divided into 2 equal numbers with a remainder of 1.

Next you pick up a shield. On the front is an instruction. This shield has a value of 100. Each time it is struck, the value reduces by 1. Modify the shield's program so its value increases with each hit.

What do you change the _ symbol to?

SHIELD = 100
IF STRUCK
THEN
SHIELD _ 2

*

GO TO PAGE 43

/

HEAD TO PAGE 27

 No! MOVE will move the original file without making a duplicate. You'd be stuck in the RAM.

TRY AGAIN
ON PAGE 19 1

 Good work! By increasing the value of the variable X to 6, you have met X > 5, which means X is larger than 5. The CPU cools down.

SPHERE takes you back to the game. The ladder's pixels are glowing brightly. You climb to the top, passing three platforms and collecting a cubie at each one. Great! Just before you reach the top, a question forms next to you.

LEVEL 1

x9

TO ACCESS THE TOP PLATFORM, WHICH IS THE ODD ONE OUT?

SAVE
GO TO PAGE 26

EXECUTE
HEAD TO PAGE 21

TIME = 9
TURN TO PAGE 12

Wrong! Although many antivirus programs contain firewalls, they have a specific job within the program.

GO BACK
TO PAGE 18

Nice work! The virus can only follow the code X = 1. When you change X to 2, the virus no longer works.

The virus starts to die and the RAM is safe. But you notice more viruses in the distance. You need to do something!

Search the files stored by the RAM for a program that can destroy all future viruses.

You look at the file list. Which do you choose?

FORMAT MEMORY

FORMAT MEMORY
GO TO PAGE 28

ANTIVIRUS

ANTIVIRUS
TURN TO PAGE 9

Correct! In 1958, American physicist William Higinbotham developed *Tennis for Two*, an early tennis video game.

You go inside the armory and collect your final cubie. Together, the cubies form a Rubik's Cube—that's your key to leaving the game!

You jump in fright as a suit of armor speaks to you.

You have nearly completed the game. Your final challenge is to face the Black Knight. Collect weapons and armor before entering the next level.

You pick up a sword and a message appears on the blade.

To activate this sword, what is the programming term modulo used for?

IT'S USED TO **COLLECT VIRUSES** AND LOCK THEM AWAY IN A DRIVE. GO TO PAGE 5

IT'S USED WHEN **CALCULATING DIVISIONS.** TURN TO PAGE 23

Wrong! You've misunderstood the algorithm.

LOOK AT IT AGAIN ON PAGE 32 **A**

No! FTP is a file transfer protocol. It is used to transfer files over a network, such as the Internet.

TRY AGAIN ON PAGE 10

 Congratulations. A Blu-ray disc can hold up to 25 gigabytes (GB) of data.

> Greetings, gamer.
> I am SPHERE. I will appear whenever your computer is in trouble and guide you to the problem. Follow me along the Program Path to the CPU (central processing unit).

You race behind SPHERE until it stops suddenly. There's a cuboid floating in front of you.

Security check
Only authorized traffic allowed on the Program Path.
What does BASIC stand for?

BEGINNER ALL-PURPOSE SYMBOLIC INSTRUCTION CODE
TURN TO PAGE 36

BINARY ALGORITHMS SAVED IN COLUMNS
GO TO PAGE 19

Amazing! HTML is used for creating web pages and controlling the formatting of text (such as color, size, and font).

SPHERE takes you back to the game and leaves you by the door to an armory.

LEVEL 3

x25

ARMORY

TO ENTER AND COLLECT THE FINAL CUBIE, ANSWER THIS QUESTION:

WHEN WAS THE FIRST VIDEO GAME INVENTED?

1920
GO TO PAGE 36

1958
TURN TO PAGE 40

No, EXECUTE is a command word that is used to run a program.

TRY AGAIN
ON PAGE 17

Incorrect. A smiley face icon might be useful for instant messaging, but it's not part of the ASCII character code.

TRY AGAIN ON PAGE 26

Correct! You chose the multiplication symbol, so every time the shield is struck, its value will double.

Finally, you approach the armor stand.

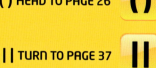

```
SHIELD = 100
IF STRUCK
THEN
SHIELD * 2
```

TO WEAR THIS ARMOR, WHICH CHARACTER IS USED IN AN "OR" ALGORITHM?

( ) HEAD TO PAGE 26 **( )**

| | TURN TO PAGE 37 **| |**

No, one petabyte equals 100,000,000 gigabytes (GB).

GO BACK TO PAGE 27 AND TRY AGAIN

Right! Bill Gates co-founded Microsoft in the 1970s with Paul Allen.

The antivirus program opens and a digital sword hovers in front of you. You examine its code to make sure that it will destroy any future viruses. There are two buttons on the sword.

```
BEGIN LOOP READ X
IF X = 0 THEN RUN SCAN
IF X = 1 THEN RUN DELETE
END LOOP READ X
```

X = 0

X = 1

Which button should you press to ensure viruses are immediately destroyed?

0 X = 0 **TURN TO PAGE 27**

1 X = 1 **HEAD TO PAGE 19**

GLOSSARY

Algorithm

A set of instructions for performing an action. For every job a computer does, it has to follow an algorithm. This is a bit like following a recipe to bake a cake.

Antivirus

A computer application that scans documents and web pages for viruses. It will also attempt to remove the virus from files, or quarantine affected files to stop them from damaging other files.

App

Short for application, an app is a program that runs on a digital device. For example, many devices have simple apps such as calculators or notepads.

RECIPE CARD

Jam Spongecake recipe

- Beat together 2 cups sugar, 2 sticks of butter, 2 cups flour, 1 tsp baking powder and 4 eggs.

- Separate the mixture into 2 cake pans and bake for 20 minutes at 350 °F until golden in color.

- Take out of the oven and leave to cool.

- Spread whipped cream and jam onto one cake, then place the other cake on top.

A recipe is a type of algorithm—it is a set of steps for performing an action.

These are some of the symbols used to represent different apps. One is for checking email. Another is a calendar.

ASCII (American Standard Code for Information Interchange)

A system used for exchanging information between computers by allowing them to recognize letters and numbers in the same way.

Binary

A numbering system that uses only 1s and 0s to represent larger numbers.

Bit

The smallest unit of data that a digital device can use, holding a value of 1 or 0.

Byte

Eight (8) bits. A unit for measuring computer information.

Command

A special word that makes a computer perform an action. For example, DELETE will remove a file from the hard drive.

CPU (central processing unit)

All digital devices come with one or more CPUs. The CPU controls what a computer does by performing calculations for applications and the operating system.

Cell phone apps perform a range of simple and more complex tasks.

Digital device

A computer, tablet, or cell phone.

Drive (SSD, HDD)

A storage device found in most digital devices. A hard disk drive (HDD) is a type of drive that spins and stores data on platters. A solid state drive (SSD) has no moving parts.

Encrypt

To protect information, such as passwords, by putting it into a special code that cannot be easily read.

Firewall

An application that protects a computer by filtering viruses and other harmful software. It also stops a computer from being looked at by people who do not have permission.

Hard drive

The part of a computer where information and programs are stored.

HTML (Hypertext Markup Language)

HTML uses special codes to create text and images in web pages.

Internet

The network of computers, servers, and mainframes that allows millions of computer users around the world to exchange information.

Loop

A special command found in many programming languages. It causes a portion of the program to repeat itself until another instruction is met.

Mainframe

The earliest type of computer, often larger than a car. Mainframes were once kept in large refrigerated rooms to prevent overheating.

Malware

A type of application or program designed to steal, copy, or observe what you do on your computer.

Pixels

Tiny dots of colored light that create digital images on a screen.

Programming

The act of creating a program to run on a digital device using special languages, such as Fortran.

Python

A type of programming language where code is typed using a keyboard. Python is easier to read than other programming languages.

RAM (random-access memory)

A type of digital storage that temporarily holds data. It can store and retrieve a computer's data in any order. When a device is turned off, data stored in RAM is lost.

Scratch

A type of programming language. Scratch uses drag-and-drop shapes that are placed in specific orders to create programs.

This shows a close-up of pixels in an image of a sunflower.

Server

The main computer that controls all other computers on the same network.

SSL (Secure Sockets Layer)

Used to allow encrypted communication between a digital device and another digital device over the Internet.

Software

Applications and programming languages that tell a computer how to do a particular job.

Terabyte (TB)

1,000 gigabytes. Many hard drives hold 3 terabytes (TB) or more of data.

UPS (uninterruptible power supply)

A large battery (or collection of batteries) that can provide power to any device plugged into it.

USB (universal serial bus)

A popular type of port found on many digital devices that allows files to be transferred or copied. USB drives are small and portable. They can be inserted into a USB port for data transfer.

USB flash drives can hold huge amounts of data.

Variable

A special character (or word) that is used to represent another value. For example, in X = 4, X is the variable and 4 is the value.

Virus

A program that damages or deletes data without the owner's permission. Other viruses are designed to steal passwords or other valuable data.

47

Taking it further

The Rubik's Quest series is designed to motivate children to develop their Science, Technology, Engineering, and Mathematics (STEM) skills. They will learn how to apply their know-how to the world through engaging adventure stories involving the Rubik's Cube, a mind-bending puzzle used throughout the world by people of all ages. For each book, readers must solve a series of problems to make progress toward the exciting conclusion.

The books do not follow a conventional pattern. The reader is directed to jump forward and backward through the book according to the answers he or she gives to the problems. If the answers are correct, the reader progresses to the next part of the story; if they are incorrect, the reason is explained before the reader is directed back to try the problem again. Additional support may be found in the glossary at the back of the book.

To support your child's development you can:

- Read the book with your child.

- Solve the initial problems and discover how the book works.

- Continue reading with your child until he or she is using the book confidently, following the "**GO TO**" instructions to find the next puzzle or explanation.

- Encourage your child to read on alone. Ask: "What's happening now?" Prompt your child to tell you how the story develops and what problems they have solved.

- Talk about the technology in your home and try to identify some of the technology mentioned in the book (such as a hard drive for a computer or laptop).

- Learn how to count to 10 in binary —here are the numbers from 0 to 10: 0000, 0001, 0010, 0011, 0100, 0101, 0110, 0111, 1000, 1001, 1010.

- Go online and learn exactly what happens inside a computer.

- Help your child work out algorithms that they could use in their daily life. Try writing a set of instructions for making a sandwich, brushing teeth, or doing a forward roll.

- Most of all, make learning fun!